D0623455

friends

A Treasury of Quotations

Illustrated by Jane Mjolsness

Running Press
PHILADELPHIA · LONDON

A Running Press Miniature Edition™

Printed in China

Library of Congress Cataloging-in-Publication Number 97-66827

ISBN 0-7624-0254-7

This book may be ordered by mail from the publisher.
Please include $1.00 for postage and handling.
But try your bookstore first!

Running Press Book Publishers
125 South Twenty-second Street
Philadelphia, Pennsylvania 19103-4399

Log onto www.specialfavors.com to order
Running Press Miniature Editions™ with
your own custom-made covers!

Contents

introduction

how do you know when a friendly stranger will become your best friend? Who will share late nights of laughter and help soothe our tears with ice cream and chocolate? What was that special moment when you knew you were best friends for life, when you found a soul mate you could trust with all your secrets?

The answer to these questions is open for debate. Friends come in all

shapes and sizes, but all are special.
They are the people who have been
with you during the fun times—and
they understand why you hate disco
music and are afraid of roller coasters.
They love you through the adventures,
and they help make the grueling times
fun—like pulling all-nighters, moving
furniture, and painting your house.

Your friends were by your side
when you built your first treehouse and
went on your first date; they were also
there with a ready hug when you didn't

land your "dream job." Friends are magical. The magic happens when two or more people become buddies, pals, amigos. It's a gift to treasure forever. Like a beautiful present, the layers of friendship are unwrapped as time goes by and the treasure grows and becomes more dear.

Collected here are memories of the joy and laughter of friends both old and new. Open these pages and share the heartfelt sentiments with the greatest people of all—your friends.

friends

forever

great friendships with women are some of life's most difficult and caring intimacies. If I work harder at them, I hope to have them forever.

—Wendy Wasserstein (b. 1950)
American playwright

*t*rue friendship is an identity
of souls rarely to be found
in the world. Only between like
natures can friendships be
altogether worthy and enduring.

—Mohandas Gandhi (1869–1948)
Indian spiritual leader

There are some friends you know you will have for the rest of your life. You're welded together by love, trust, respect, or loss—or . . . simple embarrassment.

—from *Peter's Friends*

friends

What is a friend?
A single soul dwelling
in two bodies.

—Aristotle (384–322 B.C.)
Greek philosopher

. . . "friend" covers degrees
of affection ranging
from that which emerges from
constant (and often mindless)
proximity to that which emerges
from the deepest consonances
of thought and character.

—Mary Cantwell
American editor and writer

Friendship is almost
always the union of a
part of one mind with
a part of another; peo-
ple are friends in spots.

—George Santayana (1863–1952)
Spanish-born American philosopher

*Soul-friendships
are the safety net
of the heart.*

—Susan Jeffers
American lecturer

A friend is a person who tells you all the nice things you always knew about yourself.

—Anonymous

Just thinking about a
friend makes you want
to do a happy dance,
because a friend is
someone who loves you
in spite of your faults.

—Charles M. Schulz (b. 1922)
American cartoonist

friends

*A friend is one
who walks in when
others walk out.*

—Walter Winchell (1897–1972)
American writer

i do not believe that friends
are necessarily the people
you like best, they are merely
the people who got there first.

—Peter Ustinov (b. 1921)
English actor

love the people with whom fate brings you together, but do so with all your heart.

—Marcus Aurelius (121–180)
Roman emperor and philosopher

Feelings are the connective tissue of friendship.

—Joel D. Block (b. 1943)
American writer

To the ancients, friend-
ship seemed the happiest
and most fully human of
loves; the crown of life
and the school of virtue.

—C. S. Lewis (1898–1963)
English writer

friends

*Friendship is far more
delicate than love.*

—Hester Lynch Piozzi (1741–1821)
English writer

Friendship is love
made bearable.

—Rita Mae Brown (b. 1944)
American writer

friends forever

I find friendship
to be like wine,
raw when new,
ripened with age.

—Thomas Jefferson (1743–1826)
American President

friends

*From the rocking horse
to the rocking chair,
friendship keeps teaching
us about being human.*

—Letty Cottin Pogrebin (b. 1939)
American writer

The best mirror
is an old friend.

—George Herbert (1593–1633)
English poet

Show me his friends and the man I shall know.

—Jerry Gillies (b. 1940)
American writer

the silver friend knows your present and the gold friend knows all of your past dirt and glories. Once in a blue moon there's someone who knows it all, someone who knows and accepts you unconditionally, someone who's there for life.

—Jill McCorkle (b. 1958)
American writer

*May the friends
of our youth
be the companions
of our old age.*

—Anonymous

friends
are
there
for
you

It takes a long time to
grow an old friend.

—John Leonard (b. 1939)
American critic and writer

*Friendship is a plant
which must often
be watered.*

—German proverb

We cannot tell the precise moment when friendship is formed. As in filling a vessel drop by drop there is at last a drop which makes it run over; so in a series of kindnesses there is at last one which makes the heart run over.

—James Boswell (1740–1795)
Scottish biographer

friends

If I do vow a friendship,
I'll perform it
To the last article.

—William Shakespeare (1564–1616)
English playwright and poet

friends are there for you

. . . generosity is the essence of friendship.

—Oscar Wilde (1854–1900)
Irish poet and playwright

Happiness is the by-product of an effort to make someone else happy.

—Gretta Palmer (b. 1905)
American writer

The most I can do
for my friend is simply
to be his friend.

—Henry David Thoreau (1817–1862)
American poet and writer

being a friend means
mastering the art of timing.
There is a time for silence.
A time to let go and allow people
to hurl themselves into their
own history. And a time to pick up
the pieces when it's all over.

—Gloria Naylor (b. 1950)
American writer

there was a definite process by which one made people into friends, and it involved talking to them and listening to them for hours at a time.

—Rebecca West (1892–1983)
English writer

*Friendships are fragile
things, and require
as much handling as
any other fragile and
precious thing.*

—Randolph S. Bourne (1886–1918)
American critic and pacifist

don't flatter yourself that friendship authorizes you to say disagreeable things. The nearer you come to a person, the more necessary do tact and courtesy become.

—Oliver Wendell Holmes Sr. (1809–1894)
American poet and physician

friends

It is wise to apply the oil of refined politeness to the mechanism of friendship.

—Colette [Sidonie-Gabrielle] (1873–1954)
French writer

friends are there for you

It's not what you say,
but how you say it that
makes all the difference
in human relationships.

—Hughes Mearns (1875–1965)
American writer

59

Kind words can be
short and easy to speak,
but their echoes are
truly endless.

—Mother Teresa (1910-1997)
Founder, Missionaries of Charity

i think there is a thread
that runs through each
friendship and keeps it going,
no words necessary. Each knows
what the other knows about him,
through good times and bad.

—Lauren Bacall (b. 1924)
American actress

I always felt that the great high privilege, relief, and comfort of friendship was that one had to explain nothing.

—Katherine Mansfield (1888–1923)
New Zealand-born British writer

Real friends have no problem with silence.

—Jim Lehrer (b. 1934)
American writer

You have to laugh and cry over and over again with someone before you feel comfortable.

—Joan Rivers (b. 1933)
American comic and writer

We were young to-
gether. We grew old.
Our children became adults.
But what was between us
never really changed, though
we each changed so much.

—Amanda Cross (b. 1926)
American writer

friends

*Friendship needs
a certain parallelism
of life, a community
of thought.*

—Henry Adams (1838–1918)
American historian

A truly perfect relationship is one in which each party leaves great tracts unknown in the other party.

—D. H. Lawrence (1885–1930)
English writer

The best thing to hold
onto in this world
is each other.

—Anonymous

that's

what

friends

are

for

Close friends contribute to our personal growth. They also contribute to our personal pleasure, making the music sound sweeter, the wine taste richer, the laughter ring louder because they are there.

—Judith Viorst (b. 1931)
American writer

friends

*Through knowing
her I became a better
person, and she
said the same of me.*

—Amanda Cross (b. 1926)
American writer

A friend can tell you
things you don't
want to tell yourself.

—Frances Ward Weller (b. 1935)
American writer

i guess I have been hiding. . . .
Most of my life, mostly from
myself. But you . . . you keep
blowing my cover!
You keep showing me myself.

—Elizabeth Cunningham (b. 1953)
American writer

that's what friends are for

*He makes me
feel bigger and better
than I am.*

—Wallace Stegner (1909–1993)

friends

I can no longer remain
as I was . . . you have
led me to the sunny
side, where growth
is a matter of course.

—Anna-Natalia Malachowskaja
Russian feminist

friends

Each friend represents
a world in us, a world
possibly not born until
they arrive, and it is
only by this meeting that
a new world is born.

—Anaïs Nin (1903–1977)
French-born American writer

friendship . . . can take different forms. It can run like a river, quietly and sustainingly through life; it can be an intermittent sometime thing; or it can explode like a meteor, altering the atmosphere so that nothing ever feels or looks the same again.

—Molly Haskell (b. 1939)
American critic

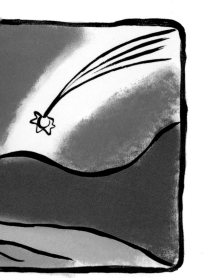

. . . thinking about our friends and our friendships forces an encounter with the ongoing evolution of one's life.

—Mickey Pearlman (b. 1938)
American writer

life is a chronicle of friendship. Friends create the world anew each day. Without their loving care, courage would not suffice to keep hearts strong for life.

—Helen Keller (1880–1968)
American writer and lecturer

*a*nd what is laughter any-
way? Changing the angle
of vision. That is what you love
a friend for: the ability to change
your angle of vision, bring
back your best self when you feel
worst, remind you of your
strengths when you feel weak.

—Erica Jong (b. 1942)
American poet and writer

best friends . . . show us we
have separate lives. They
offer us affection solely for who
we are, surprise us with the
scope of another's existence. . . .

—Valerie Schultz
American writer

There's a kind of
emotional exploration
you plumb with a
friend that you
don't really do with
your family.

—Bette Midler (b. 1945)
American singer, actor, and writer

that's what friends are for

. . . no friendship can
cross the path of our
destiny without leaving
some mark on it forever.

—Francois Mauriac (1885–1970)
French playwright

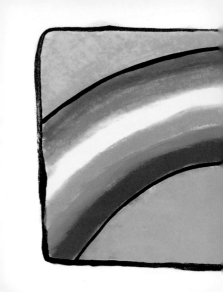

friends

One sees much more

in a friend.

—Saul Bellow (b. 1915)
Canadian-born American writer

that's what friends are for

It's the friends you
can call up at 4 A.M.
that matter.

—Marlene Dietrich (1901–1992)
German-born American actress and singer

I have learned that
to be with those I like
is enough.

—Walt Whitman (1819–1892)
American writer

there were equal measures
of comfort and amusement
in our communications;
I think it is safe to say that we
delighted in one another.
She used to laugh at my stories
until she wept, and I tried
to take her sound advice to heart.

—Jane Hamilton (b. 1957)
American writer

friends

*Savor the moments
that are warm
and special and giggly.*

—Sammy Davis Jr. (1925–1990)
American entertainer

One of the sweetest
things in life:
a letter from a friend.

—Andy Rooney
American television commentator

*Happiness is having
a friend to curl up with.*

—Patricia Curtis (b. 1924)
American writer

Friendship doubles our joy and divides our grief.

—Cicero (106–43 B.C.)
Roman orator and writer

Friendship is
certainly the finest balm
for the pangs
of disappointed love.

— Jane Austen (1775–1817)
English writer

*Friendship is the only
cement that will ever
hold the world together.*

—Woodrow Wilson (1856–1924)
American President

Do not protect yourself
by a fence but,
rather by your friends.

—Czech proverb

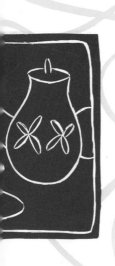

with
a little
help
from
our
friends

"Why did you do all this for me?" he asked. "I don't deserve it. I've never done anything for you."

"You have been my friend," replied Charlotte. "That in itself is a tremendous thing."

—E. B. White (1899–1985)
American writer

with a little help from our friends

Everyone needs help from everyone.

—Bertolt Brecht (1898–1956)
German playwright and poet

"Friendship,"
said Christopher Robin,
"is a very comforting
thing to have."

—A. A. Milne (1882–1956)
English poet and writer

friends

. . . the best relief from
life was the presence
of a friend who seldom
asked us for more
than we could give.

—Barbara Raskin (b. 1935)
American writer

Friends seem to be like aspirin: we don't really know why they make a sick person feel better but they do.

—Letty Cottin Pogrebin (b. 1939)
American writer

friends

*Friendship takes fear
from the heart.*

—-from *The Mahabharata*

It seems to me that trying
to live without friends is
like milking a bear to get cream
for your morning coffee.
It is a whole lot of trouble,
and then not worth
much after you get it.

—Zora Neale Hurston (1903–1960)
American writer

*It is a good thing to
be rich, and a good thing
to be strong, but it is
a better thing to be
beloved of many friends.*

—Euripides (c. 484·406 B.C.)
Greek playwright

*If I don't have friends,
then I ain't got nothin'.*

—Billie Holiday (1915–1959)
American singer

with a little help from our friends

True happiness consists
not in the multitude
of friends but in their
worth and choice.

—Ben Johnson (b. 1940)
American writer

friends

So long as we are loved
by others I should say that
we are almost indispensable;
and no man is useless
while he has a friend.

—Robert Louis Stevenson (1850–1894)
English writer

The friends of our friends are our friends.

—African proverb

friends

Snowflakes are one of
nature's most fragile things,
but just look what they
do when they stick together.

—Verna M. Kelly
American writer

126

with a little help from our friends

Friendship?
Yes, please.

—Charles Dickens (1812–1870)
English writer

This book has been bound using handcraft methods, and is Smyth-sewn to ensure durability.

The cover and interior were illustrated by Jane Mjolsness.

The dust jacket and interior were designed by Corinda Cook.

The text was edited by Glenda M. Insua.

The text was set in Footlight and Spring.